FOUR MINOR TIMELINES

THE ZENIFF TIMELINE

200 BC

A Nephite named Zeniff takes his followers to reclaim the land of their "first inheritance."

THE ALMA TIMELINE

147 BC

A wicked priest named Alma is converted unto the Lord and leads a group of righteous followers to a land called Helam.

HIMNI   OMNER   AMMON   AARON

THE SONS OF MOSIAH TIMELINE

91 BC

The four sons of Mosiah, the last Nephite prophet-king, become missionaries to the Lamanites.

THE ALMA THE YOUNGER TIMELINE

83 BC

Alma, son of Alma, resigns as chief judge and leaves a land called Zarahemla to teach in other Nephite cities.

AD 1830

The record, translated into English by the Prophet Joseph Smith, is published as the Book of Mormon.

THE BOOK OF MORMON TIMELINE

BY MORGAN CHOI
ART BY JOYNEVADA

DESERET BOOK

2500–2200 BC

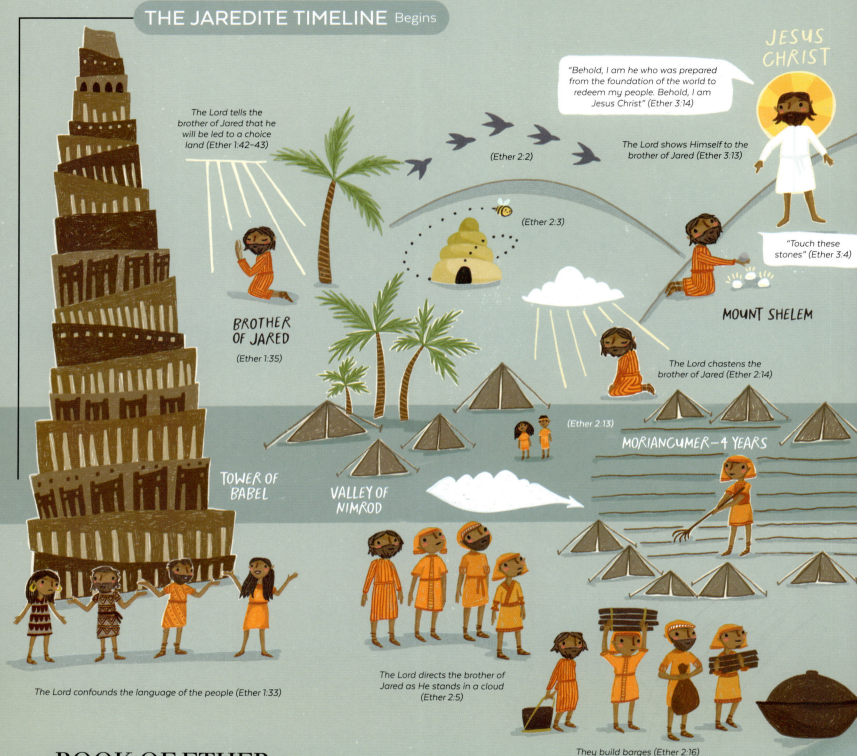

THE JAREDITE TIMELINE Begins

"Behold, I am he who was prepared from the foundation of the world to redeem my people. Behold, I am Jesus Christ" (Ether 3:14)

JESUS CHRIST

The Lord tells the brother of Jared that he will be led to a choice land (Ether 1:42–43)

(Ether 2:2)

The Lord shows Himself to the brother of Jared (Ether 3:13)

(Ether 2:3)

"Touch these stones" (Ether 3:4)

BROTHER OF JARED (Ether 1:35)

MOUNT SHELEM

The Lord chastens the brother of Jared (Ether 2:14)

(Ether 2:13)

MORIANCUMER – 4 YEARS

TOWER OF BABEL

VALLEY OF NIMROD

The Lord confounds the language of the people (Ether 1:33)

The Lord directs the brother of Jared as He stands in a cloud (Ether 2:5)

They build barges (Ether 2:16)

The BOOK OF ETHER

Thousands of years before the birth of Christ, descendants of Noah become wicked and build a great tower known as the Tower of Babel. Because of their wickedness, the Lord confounds their language (Genesis 11:4–9; Ether 1:33). A man known as the brother of Jared asks the Lord to preserve his language and the language of his family and his friends (Ether 1:34–37). The Lord is merciful to the brother of Jared and answers his prayers by instructing him to build barges so he and his family and friends can travel across the ocean to a promised land. The Lord instructs the brother of Jared to keep a record (Ether 3:22). After arriving in the promised land, the brother of Jared and his people, known as the Jaredites, prosper (Ether 6:18). Despite warnings from the brother of Jared, the Jaredites choose a king (Ether 6:22–27). The first Jaredite king, Orihah, reigns in righteousness (Ether 7:1).

The FIRST BOOK OF NEPHI

About 600 years before the birth of Christ, a man named Nephi begins a record of his people. The people living in Jerusalem are wicked (1 Nephi 1:4). Nephi's father, a prophet named Lehi, calls them to repentance, but they become angry and seek to kill him (1 Nephi 1:20). The Lord commands Lehi to take his family and leave Jerusalem (1 Nephi 2:2). Lehi's sons return to Jerusalem to obtain the brass plates, which contain a record of the Jews from the creation of the world to the commencement of the reign of Zedekiah, king of Judah (1 Nephi 5:11–13). A man named Zoram (1 Nephi 4:32–35) as well as a man named Ishmael and his family (1 Nephi 7:2–5) join Lehi and his growing family in the wilderness (1 Nephi 18:7). They cross the ocean in a ship that the Lord commands Nephi to build (1 Nephi 17:8) and arrive in the same promised land (1 Nephi 18:23) where the Lord led the Jaredites hundreds of years earlier (Ether 6:12). A man named Mulek, a son of Zedekiah (Helaman 6:10), leaves Jerusalem around the same time as Lehi and his family. His descendants—later known as the people of Zarahemla—and the righteous descendants of Lehi eventually meet and unite together in the promised land (Omni 1:15, 19).

600 BC   600–592 BC

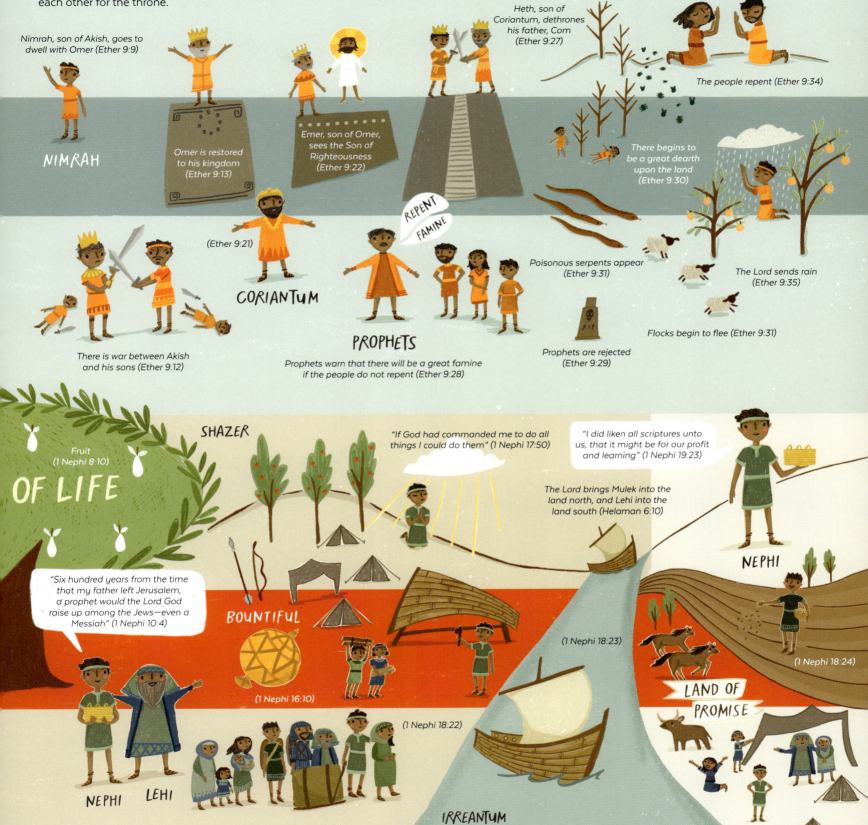

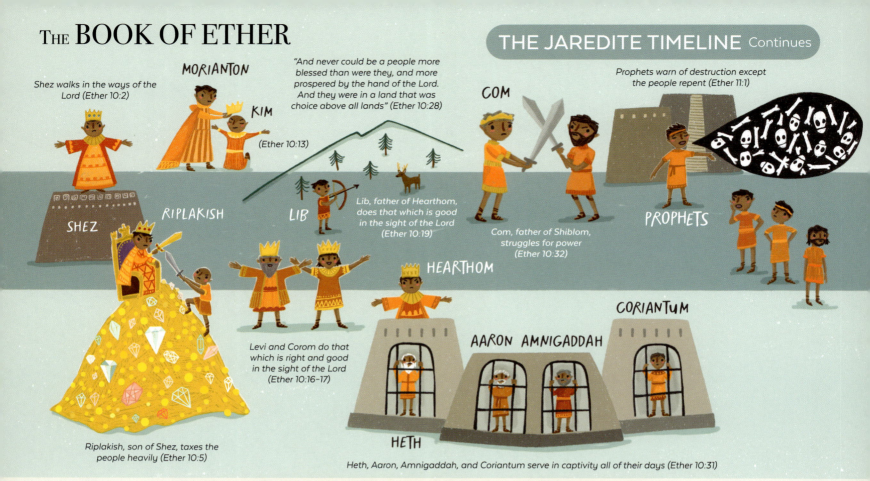

THE SECOND BOOK OF NEPHI

In the promised land, Lehi gathers his family and blesses them before he dies. He repeatedly emphasizes to his family that the Lord will bless and prosper them if they keep His commandments (2 Nephi 1:7, 9, 20, 32; 3:2; 4:4). Lehi pleads with Laman and Lemuel not to rebel against their younger brother Nephi (2 Nephi 1:24, 28), but after Lehi's death (2 Nephi 4:12), Laman and Lemuel become angry with Nephi (2 Nephi 4:13) and seek to kill him (2 Nephi 5:2-3). The Lord warns Nephi to flee into the wilderness (2 Nephi 5:5). He takes the records and all those who choose to follow him to a place they call Nephi (2 Nephi 5:6-8). They become known as the Nephites, and the brothers they flee from become known as the Lamanites (Jacob 1:14). The Nephites keep the commandments of the Lord (2 Nephi 5:10) and prosper exceedingly in the land (2 Nephi 5:11).

588–570 BC   588–559 BC   559–545 BC

The BOOK OF JACOB

Nephi becomes old and his younger brother, Jacob, who was born in the wilderness (1 Nephi 18:7), is commanded to continue the record (Jacob 1:1-2). Before Nephi dies (Jacob 1:12), he anoints a man as king and ruler over his people (Jacob 1:9). Under the second king, the Nephites grow hard in their hearts and indulge in wicked practices (Jacob 1:15-16). The Lord commands Jacob to call them to repentance (Jacob 2:9, 11). Jacob warns the Nephites that if they don't repent, their brethren, the Lamanites, will possess the land of their inheritance (Jacob 3:3-4). A man named Sherem comes among the Nephites and declares there will be no Christ (Jacob 7:1-2). He asks Jacob for a sign (Jacob 7:13) and is smitten by God (Jacob 7:15). Before his death, Sherem admits he had been deceived by the devil and bears witness of the reality of Christ (Jacob 7:17-20).

544-421 BC

500–250 BC

The BOOK OF ETHER

Coriantumr is king over all the land (Ether 12:1) and repents not (Ether 13:22). After he witnesses the destruction of the Jaredites, he is discovered by the people of Zarahemla (Omni 1:21). Ether, the last Jaredite prophet, finishes the record of the Jaredites, which is later incorporated into the Book of Mormon as the book of Ether. Ether hides the record (Ether 15:33), which is discovered many years later by a group of Nephites known as the people of Limhi (Mosiah 21:26–27).

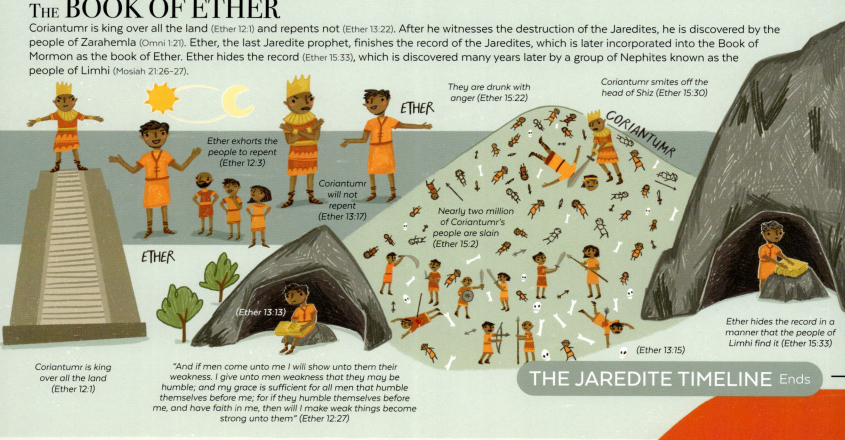

Coriantumr is king over all the land (Ether 12:1)

Ether exhorts the people to repent (Ether 12:3)

Coriantumr will not repent (Ether 13:17)

They are drunk with anger (Ether 15:22)

Coriantumr smites off the head of Shiz (Ether 15:30)

Nearly two million of Coriantumr's people are slain (Ether 15:2)

(Ether 13:13)

(Ether 13:15)

Ether hides the record in a manner that the people of Limhi find it (Ether 15:33)

"And if men come unto me I will show unto them their weakness. I give unto men weakness that they may be humble; and my grace is sufficient for all men that humble themselves before me; for if they humble themselves before me, and have faith in me, then will I make weak things become strong unto them" (Ether 12:27)

THE JAREDITE TIMELINE Ends

The BOOK OF JAROM

The record is passed to Jarom, son of Enos, who also witnesses wars between the Nephites and Lamanites. Leaders mighty in faith teach the Nephites, helping them prosper and withstand the attacks of the Lamanites (Jarom 1:7–9). The Nephites are spared from destruction.

"Thy sins are forgiven thee . . . because of thy faith in Christ" (Enos 1:5, 8)

Enos prays to God (Enos 1:4)

(Enos 1:19)

Enos sees wars between the Nephites and Lamanites (Enos 1:24)

LAND OF NEPHI

The Nephites withstand the Lamanites (Jarom 1:6–7)

(Jarom 1:1)

The BOOK OF ENOS

The record is passed to Enos, son of Jacob, who goes to the forest to hunt beasts and remembers the words his father spoke concerning eternal life (Enos 1:3). He prays all day long and into the night for a remission of sins (Enos 1:4) and hears the voice of the Lord telling him that his sins are forgiven (Enos 1:5) because of his faith in Christ (Enos 1:8). The Nephites strive to restore the Lamanites to the truth but are not successful (Enos 1:20). Enos witnesses wars between the Nephites and Lamanites (Enos 1:24).

420 BC

399–361 BC

The BOOK OF OMNI

The record is passed down the family line to a man named Amaleki, who records how a Nephite named Mosiah was warned by the Lord to depart from the land of Nephi and flee into the wilderness (Omni 1:12). In the wilderness, Mosiah and his followers discover the people of Zarahemla, also known as the Mulekites. They rejoice to find that Mosiah has the plates of brass (Omni 1:14). They unite with Mosiah and his followers and Mosiah becomes king (Omni 1:19). Mosiah learns that Coriantumr dwelt with the people of Zarahemla for nine moons (Omni 1:21; the book of Ether). After Mosiah dies, his son, Benjamin, reigns in his stead (Omni 1:23). Having no children, Amaleki gives the records to King Benjamin (Omni 1:25).

Coriantumr was discovered by the people of Zarahemla (Omni 1:21)

THE NEPHITE TIMELINE Combines with the People of Zarahemla

CORIANTUMR

KING MOSIAH

(Omni 1:25)
KING BENJAMIN

MOSIAH
The Lord warns Mosiah to depart out of the land of Nephi (Omni 1:12)

The people of Zarahemla and Mosiah unite together and Mosiah is appointed king (Omni 1:19)

ZENIFF

The people of Zarahemla, also known as the Mulekites, left Jerusalem around the same time as Lehi and his family (Omni 1:15)

A man named Zeniff leaves the land of Zarahemla with a large number of people to possess the land of Nephi, the land of their inheritance (Omni 1:27–29)

"And now, my beloved brethren, I would that ye should come unto Christ" (Omni 1:26)

(Jarom 1:15) (Omni 1:3) (Omni 1:8) (Omni 1:10) (Omni 1:12)
JAROM OMNI AMARON CHEMISH ABINADOM AMALEKI

323–130 BC

The WORDS OF MORMON

King Benjamin is a holy man and reigns in righteousness (Words of Mormon 1:17). He faces contentions among his own people (Words of Mormon 1:12) and wars with the Lamanites but is able to drive the Lamanites out of the land (Words of Mormon 1:14). With the help of holy prophets, he reestablishes peace (Words of Mormon 1:17–18).

(Words of Mormon 1:10)

LAND OF ZARAHEMLA

KING BENJAMIN

King Benjamin has contentions among his own people (Words of Mormon 1:12)

King Benjamin gathers together his armies, stands against the Lamanites, and fights with the strength of his own arm (Words of Mormon 1:13)

THE ZENIFF TIMELINE Begins

ZENIFF

KING LAMAN

LAND OF LEHI-NEPHI

The Lamanites have an eternal hatred toward the children of Nephi (Mosiah 10:17)

It is the cunning and craftiness of King Laman to bring Zeniff's people into bondage (Mosiah 9:10)

(Mosiah 9:9)

(Mosiah 9:18–19)

LAND OF SHILOM

279 NEPHITES

3,043 LAMANITES

The BOOK OF MOSIAH

A group of people led by a man named Zeniff leaves Zarahemla to return to the land of Nephi (Omni 1:27–29). They enter into a treaty with Laman, king of the Lamanites, who deceives Zeniff by giving him and his followers a part of the land (Mosiah 7:21–22). The people in the land of Nephi choose Zeniff to be their king (Mosiah 7:9). The Lamanites attack Zeniff's people to bring them into bondage (Mosiah 9:14) but are driven out of the land (Mosiah 10:20). Zeniff confers his kingdom upon Noah, one of his sons (Mosiah 10:22; 11:1). Noah is a wicked king (Mosiah 11:1–15). A prophet named Abinadi warns King Noah that if he doesn't repent, he and his people will be delivered into the hands of the Lamanites (Mosiah 11:21). King Noah commands that Abinadi be put to death (Mosiah 17:1) but Abinadi, protected by divine power, delivers a mighty testimony of the Savior (Mosiah 12–16) before suffering death by fire. Alma, a young priest of King Noah, believes Abinadi's words and tries to defend him (Mosiah 17:2). King Noah casts Alma out and sends his servants to kill him (Mosiah 17:3) but Alma escapes (Mosiah 17:4).

200–187 BC   187–160 BC

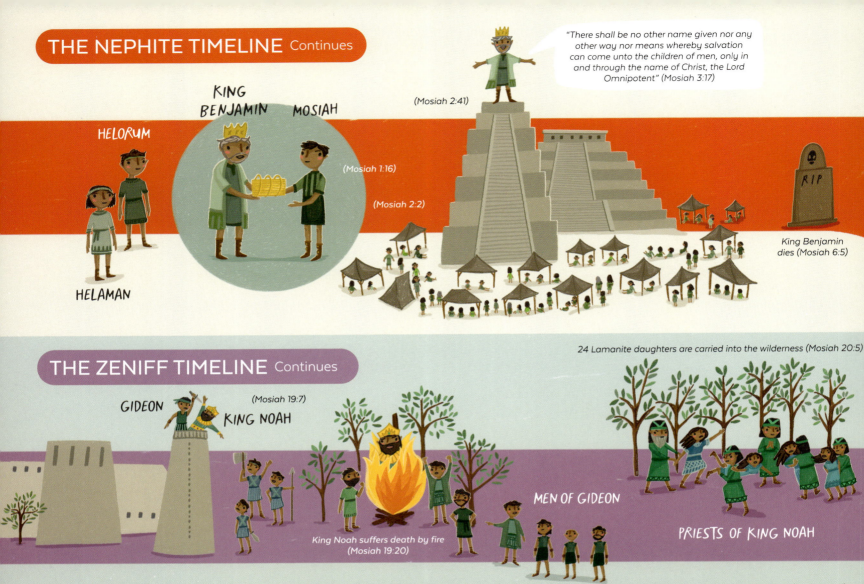

The Lamanites attack King Noah and his people (Mosiah 19:9–10). King Noah flees with his wicked priests and commands his people to leave behind their wives and children (Mosiah 19:11). Some who follow his orders are later angry with King Noah and burn him to death (Mosiah 19:20). Others who choose to stay with their wives and children, including Limhi, a son of King Noah, are placed in bondage and forced to pay tribute to the Lamanites (Mosiah 19:26), who continue to persecute them (Mosiah 21:1–3). Limhi becomes their king (Mosiah 19:26–27). King Limhi meets Ammon and his brethren, who were sent to the land of Nephi by King Mosiah. Ammon and King Limhi consult with the people and come up with a plan to escape (Mosiah 22:1, 5–9). They gather their flocks and precious things and secretly depart from the land of Nephi by night (Mosiah 22:11). After many days in the wilderness, they arrive in the land of Zarahemla and join the people of King Mosiah (Mosiah 22:13).

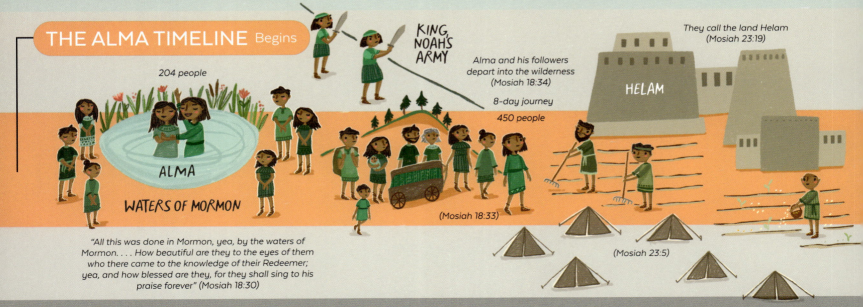

147 BC

The BOOK OF MOSIAH

King Benjamin gives his oldest son, Mosiah, the records and puts him in charge of all the affairs of the kingdom (Mosiah 1:15-16). Before he dies, King Benjamin has a tower erected from which he speaks to his people (Mosiah 2:7). He testifies of Jesus Christ, the Son of God, who will minister among men and atone for the sins of the world (Mosiah 3:5-11). King Benjamin's people feel the Spirit, or Holy Ghost, and believe in the truthfulness of his words (Mosiah 5:2). They enter into a covenant to do the Lord's will and obey His commandments (Mosiah 5:5-7). King Mosiah desires to know what happened to Zeniff and his people (Mosiah 7:1). He sends Ammon and 15 other men to the land of Lehi-Nephi (Mosiah 7:2-3), where they discover King Limhi, grandson of Zeniff, and his people in bondage to the Lamanites (Mosiah 7:15).

After Alma repents (Mosiah 18:1-2), he teaches and baptizes people in secret at a place called Mormon (Mosiah 18:3-4, 16). When King Noah finds out, he sends an army to stop him, but Alma and hundreds of his followers escape into the wilderness (Mosiah 18:34-35) and settle in a beautiful and pleasant land, which they call Helam (Mosiah 23:4-5, 19). The Lamanites take possession of the land of Helam (Mosiah 23:29) and make Amulon, once a priest of King Noah, a ruler over Alma and his people (Mosiah 23:39). Amulon persecutes them (Mosiah 24:8). Alma and his people pray mightily to the Lord (Mosiah 24:10), and the Lord lightens their burdens (Mosiah 24:14-15). With the help of the Lord, Alma and his people escape to the land of Zarahemla (Mosiah 24:19-21), where King Mosiah and his people receive them with joy (Mosiah 24:25).

120 BC

The sons of Mosiah are numbered among the unbelievers (Mosiah 27:8)

SONS OF MOSIAH

Alma and the priests fast and pray to the Lord their God that Alma the Younger's mouth will be opened and that his limbs will receive their strength (Mosiah 27:22)

REIGN OF THE JUDGES

The Nephites appoint judges to rule over them (Mosiah 29:41)

ALMA THE YOUNGER

"Alma, arise and stand forth, for why persecutest thou the church of God?" (Mosiah 27:13)

(Mosiah 29:45) (Mosiah 29:46)

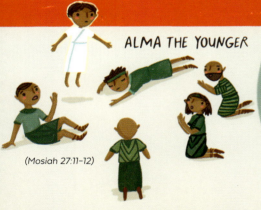

ALMA THE YOUNGER

(Mosiah 27:11-12)

Alma the Younger sees an angel and his astonishment is so great that he becomes weak and unable to speak. (Mosiah 27:19)

(Mosiah 28:20)

KING MOSIAH   ALMA THE YOUNGER

HIMNI   OMNER   AMMON   AARON

(Mosiah 28:3)

They take their journey into the wilderness to go up to preach the word among the Lamanites (Mosiah 28:9)

The BOOK OF MOSIAH

King Mosiah and his people unite with the people of Limhi and the people of Alma in the land of Zarahemla. There is peace for a time but many of the rising generation, those who were too young to understand the words of King Benjamin, do not believe the traditions of their fathers (Mosiah 26:1-4). Among the disbelievers are Alma's son, known as Alma the Younger, and the four sons of Mosiah, who lead the people astray (Mosiah 27:8-9). Alma prays with much faith for his son, and in response to his prayers (Mosiah 27:14), an angel appears to Alma the Younger and the sons of Mosiah (Mosiah 27:11). Alma the Younger is greatly astonished and becomes weak and speechless (Mosiah 27:19). He repents and recovers (Mosiah 27:23-24) and, along with the sons of Mosiah, proclaims the word of God (Mosiah 27:32). After teaching the Nephites, the sons of Mosiah ask for and receive permission from their father, King Mosiah, to preach to the Lamanites (Mosiah 28:5-8). The Lord promises King Mosiah that his sons will be successful and protected (Mosiah 28:7). King Mosiah proposes to his people a system of judges to replace the reign of kings (Mosiah 29:11). Before he dies, King Mosiah passes the records to Alma the Younger (Mosiah 28:20), who is appointed as the first chief judge (Mosiah 29:42-44) in the land of Zarahemla. There is peace throughout the land (Mosiah 29:43).

100-92 BC   92-91 BC

THE NEPHITE TIMELINE Continues

The BOOK OF ALMA
A man named Nehor is brought before Alma the Younger, the chief judge, for teaching false doctrine among the Nephites (Alma 1:2–10) and for slaying a righteous man named Gideon (Alma 1:7–9). Nehor is sentenced to death (Alma 1:12–14) but this doesn't stop priestcraft from spreading. Amlici, a cunning, wicked man, attracts many followers (Alma 2:1–2), who make him their king (Alma 2:9). Amlici leads his men to war against the Nephites (Alma 2:14). The Nephites slay and pursue the Amlicites, but to their great astonishment, the Amlicites join forces with the Lamanites (Alma 2:17–18, 24–25). Strengthened by the Lord, the Nephites defeat the Lamanites and the Amlicites (Alma 2:28, 35) and live in peace for a time (Alma 4:5), but their prosperity leads to pride (Alma 4:6–12), and Alma admonishes them to repent (Alma 5:50–51, 62).

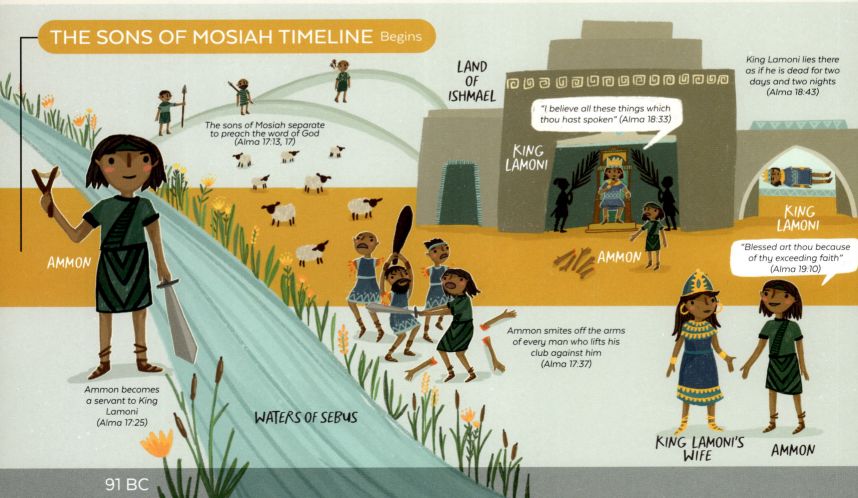

THE SONS OF MOSIAH TIMELINE Begins

91 BC

90–77 BC

The BOOK OF ALMA

Alma delivers up the judgment seat to Nephihah and focuses wholly on being high priest over the church of God (Alma 4:16-20). He sets in order the church in the city of Zarahemla (Alma 6:4), preaches in the lands of Gideon and Melek, and is rejected in the city of Ammonihah (Alma 8:9-13). He is cast out of the city but an angel commands him to return (Alma 8:14-16). The angel also commands a man named Amulek to receive and feed Alma (Alma 8:20, 27). Alma and Amulek preach repentance to the people of Ammonihah (Alma 8:30-32) and contend with a wicked man named Zeezrom (Alma 11:21-46) who later repents (Alma 14:7) and is baptized (Alma 15:12). Most of the people are angry with Alma and Amulek because they testify plainly of their wickedness (Alma 14:2-3). Alma and Amulek are forced to watch as the believers are cast into a fire (Alma 14:8-9). Alma and Amulek are cast into prison (Alma 14:18), but God delivers them by causing the prison walls to fall (Alma 14:28). Alma returns to the land of Zarahemla (Alma 15:18).

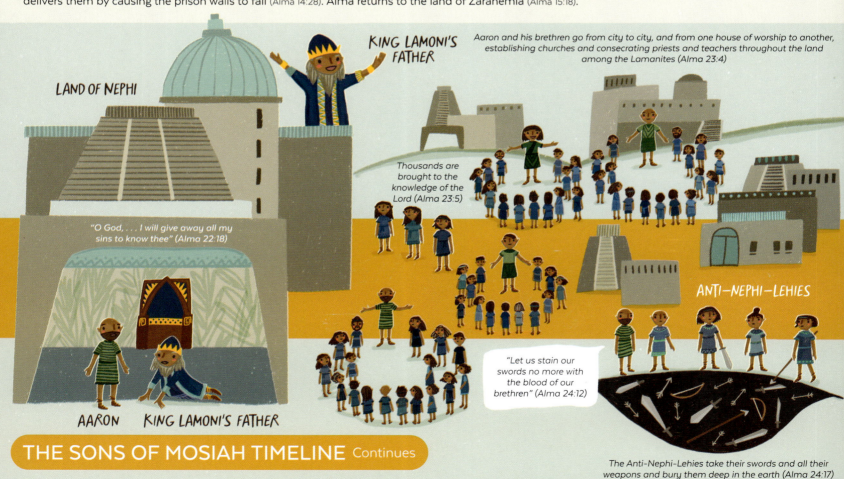

THE SONS OF MOSIAH TIMELINE Continues

90-77 BC

THE BOOK OF ALMA

A man named Korihor, an anti-Christ, comes into the land of Zarahemla and preaches that there should be no Christ (Alma 30:6, 12–18). Korihor asks Alma for a sign to convince him there is a God (Alma 30:43) and loses his ability to speak (Alma 30:50). He goes forth among a group of apostate Nephites called the Zoramites and is trodden down and killed (Alma 30:56–59). Alma heads a mission to teach the Zoramites (Alma 31:5–7). Many poor Zoramites who believe in the words of Alma and his brethren are cast out and join the people of Ammon in the land of Jershon (Alma 35:6). Alma gives his oldest son, Helaman, the records (Alma 37:1). A man named Moroni is appointed chief captain of the Nephites (Alma 43:16). The Nephite army fights and defeats the Lamanites (Alma 43:34–54; 44:1–20), who are led by a man named Zerahemnah (Alma 43:5). In the days of Helaman, a large and cunning man named Amalickiah seeks to destroy the church and the foundation of liberty (Alma 46:3, 10). He uses flattery to lead the Nephites away from God (Alma 46:5–7). Captain Moroni rallies the people by waving a torn part of his coat, called the title of liberty, in the air and proclaiming that if the Nephites want to maintain their rights and religion, they must covenant with God to keep His commandments (Alma 46:19–21). Amalickiah uses deceit, murder, and trickery to become king of the Lamanites (Alma 47:1–35).

| 74–73 BC | 72 BC | 72–67 BC |

THE BOOK OF ALMA

In Zarahemla, a man named Pahoran is appointed to fill the judgment seat after his father, Nephihah (Alma 50:39–40). There is contention (Alma 51:2-4) between king-men, who desire to overthrow the free government and establish a king (Alma 51:5), and freemen, who want Pahoran to remain chief judge over the land (Alma 51:6). Amalickiah, king of the Lamanites, takes possession of many Nephite cities (Alma 51:26-27) but is killed by a Nephite warrior named Teancum (Alma 51:33-34). Ammoron, Amalickiah's brother, is appointed king of the Lamanites (Alma 52:3). The Nephites and Lamanites continue to battle. When the people of Ammon see the afflictions and tribulations the Nephites bear to protect them, they want to fight (Alma 53:10-13), but Helaman persuades them to keep their oath renouncing bloodshed (Alma 15:14-15). Their sons, however, who are not bound by such an oath, covenant to protect the land and fight for the liberty of the Nephites (Alma 53:16-17). There are 2,000 of them (Alma 53:18). They choose Helaman to be their leader (Alma 53:19) and they fight with mighty power and miraculous strength (Alma 56:56). The king-men drive out Pahoran from the judgment seat and take the city of Zarahemla (Alma 61:5, 8). Moroni raises the standard of liberty to gather support for Pahoran and his army of freemen (Alma 62:4-6). They defeat the king-men and Pahoran is restored to his judgment seat (Alma 62:6-8). The sacred records are passed from Helaman to Shiblon (Alma 63:1), and then to Helaman, son of Helaman (Alma 63:11).

67–66 BC   66–64 BC

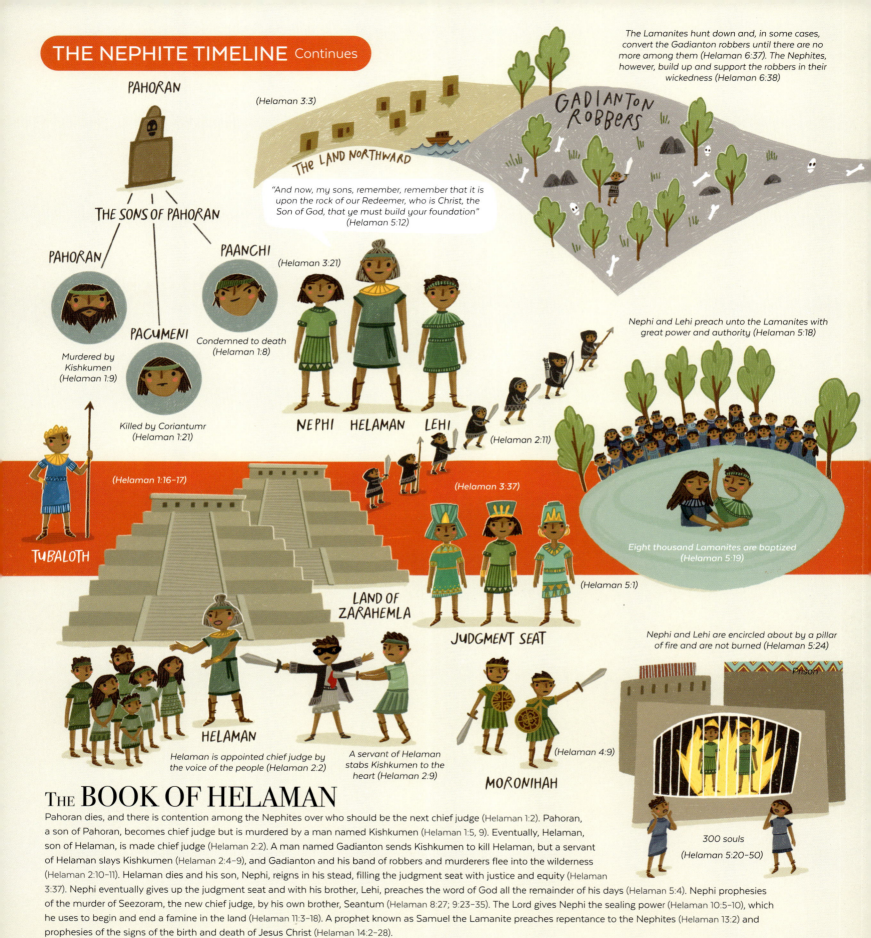

THIRD NEPHI

Nephi, son of Helaman, passes the sacred records to his son, Nephi (3 Nephi 1:2). The night of Christ's birth arrives, and a new star appears, as prophesied by Samuel the Lamanite (3 Nephi 1:19–21). Wickedness increases among the people, and the Nephites and Lamanites unite to defend themselves against the Gadianton robbers (3 Nephi 2:3, 12). Nephi preaches repentance and remission of sins through faith in the Lord Jesus Christ (3 Nephi 7:15–16). Thirty-three years after the birth of Christ, many people are destroyed by tempests, earthquakes, fires, whirlwinds, and physical upheavals, which last for about three hours (3 Nephi 8:2–19). Thick darkness covers the land for three days (3 Nephi 8:20–23). A great multitude gathers around the temple in the land Bountiful (3 Nephi 11:1). While they converse with one another about Jesus Christ, they hear a small voice, which causes their hearts to burn (3 Nephi 11:2–3). The Father testifies of His Beloved Son (3 Nephi 11:7). Christ appears and invites the people to thrust their hands into His side and feel the prints of the nails in His hands and in His feet (3 Nephi 11:8–15). He calls twelve disciples (3 Nephi 12:1) and announces that the law of Moses is fulfilled in Him (3 Nephi 15:2–10). He blesses their little children (3 Nephi 17:21–23) and teaches the people (3 Nephi 26:1–4).

AD 1   AD 16–18   AD 33–34

THE NEPHITE TIMELINE Continues

There is thick darkness upon all the face of the land for three days (3 Nephi 8:20-23)

"Behold my Beloved Son, in whom I am well pleased, in whom I have glorified my name—hear ye him" (3 Nephi 11:7)

Jesus takes their little children, one by one, and blesses them, and prays unto the Father for them (3 Nephi 17:21)

THE TWELVE DISCIPLES
The twelve disciples are chosen (3 Nephi 12:1)

BEHOLD, I AM JESUS CHRIST, WHOM THE PROPHETS TESTIFIED SHALL COME INTO THE WORLD (3 Nephi 11:10)

BEATITUDES
(3 Nephi 12:3-12)

"Blessed are the poor in spirit who come unto me, for theirs is the kingdom of heaven" (3 Nephi 12:3)

"Therefore I would that ye should be perfect even as I, or your Father who is in heaven is perfect" (3 Nephi 12:48)

THE THREE NEPHITES

(3 Nephi 28:4-7)

NEPHI

The people see a man in a white robe descending out of heaven. He comes down and stands in the midst of them (3 Nephi 11:8)

(3 Nephi 11:12)

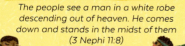

Those baptized in the name of Christ are called the church of Christ (3 Nephi 26:21)

AD 34

AD 34-35

FOURTH NEPHI

The Nephites and Lamanites are all converted unto the Lord (4 Nephi 1:1–2). There is no contention in the land because the people have the love of God in their hearts (4 Nephi 1:15). Three hundred years after the birth of Christ, both the Nephites and the Lamanites become very wicked (4 Nephi 1:45). The Gadianton robbers spread over all the face of the land (4 Nephi 1:46). The sacred records are passed from Nephi to his son Amos, to his son Amos, to his brother, Ammaron, who is instructed by the Holy Ghost to hide the records (4 Nephi 1:19, 21, 47–48).

TO IVY AND MARGARET

Text © 2023 Morgan Choi
Illustrations © 2023 JoyNevada

All rights reserved. No part of this book may be reproduced in any form or by any means without permission in writing from the publisher, Deseret Book Company, at permissions@deseretbook.com. This work is not an official publication of The Church of Jesus Christ of Latter-day Saints. The views expressed herein are the responsibility of the author and do not necessarily represent the position of the Church or of Deseret Book Company.

Deseret Book is a registered trademark of Deseret Book Company.

Visit us at deseretbook.com

Library of Congress Cataloging-in-Publication Data
(CIP data on file)
ISBN 978-1-63993-228-3

Printed in the United States of America   9/2023
PubLitho, Clarksville, TN
10 9 8 7 6 5 4 3 2 1